Sri Durga Chalisa

Written by : Sant Devidas

Presented by: Divinebharat

Art by: Sujata Saha

Written by : Sant Devidas
Presented by: Divinebharat
Art by: Sujata Saha

ISBN:978-93-343-2588-1
For enquiries, contact:
info.divinebharat@gmail.com

www.divinebharat.co

Introduction

The Sri **Durga Chalisa** is a sacred hymn composed in forty verses (chaupais) dedicated to **Maa Durga**, the Divine Mother and embodiment of Shakti (cosmic power). This powerful devotional composition extols the various forms, deeds, and divine attributes of the Goddess, invoking her grace for protection, prosperity, wisdom, and spiritual liberation.

Traditionally attributed to **Sant Devidas**, the Chalisa reflects deep devotion, poetic richness, and spiritual insight. It draws upon stories from the *Devī Māhātmya*, *Puranas*, and various folk traditions, celebrating Mā Durga's victories over demons like Mahishasura, Shumbha, Nishumbha, and Raktabīja — symbolizing the triumph of righteousness over evil, light over darkness, and divine order over chaos.

Reciting the Durgā Chālīsā with **faith and regularity** is believed to:

- Remove fears and obstacles
- Bring peace, courage, and clarity
- Bestow material and spiritual well-being
- Grant divine protection in times of distress

Devotees often chant it during **Navratri**, on **Tuesdays and Fridays**,or as part of their daily spiritual practice. Its verses are filled with devotion (bhakti), surrender (sharaṇagati), and the glorification of the universal mother who nourishes, protects, and liberates her children.

This book presents the **full** S**ri Durga Chalisa** in, **Roman transliteration**,, making it accessible to readers of all backgrounds. Whether you are new to chanting or a lifelong devotee, this Chalisa will bring you closer to the divine energy that is ever-present and ever-compassionate — **Maa Jagadamba Durga**.

Sri Durga Chalisa

Namo Namo Durge Sukh Karni |

Namo Namo Ambe Dukh Harni ||1||

Nirankar Hai Jyoti Tumhari |

Tihu Lok Phale Ujiyari ||2||

Shashi Lalat Mukh Mahavishala |

Naitra Lal Brukuti Vikrala ||3||

Roop Matu Ko Adhik Suhavey |

Darash Karat Jan Ati Sukhpavay ||4||

Tum Sansar Shakti Lai Kina |

Paalan Hetu Ann Dhan Dina ||5||

Annpoorna Hui Jag Paala |

Tum Hi Aadi Sundari Baala ||6||

Pralaykaal Sab Naashan Haari |

Tum Gauri Shiv Shankar Pyari ||7||

Shiv Yogi Tumharey Gun Gavey |

Brahma Vishnu Tumhe Nit Dhyavey ||8||

Roop Saraswati Ko Tum Dhaara |

De Subuddhi Rishi Munin Ubaara ||9||

Dharaa Roop Narsinh Ko Amba |

Pargat Bhayin Phaad Kar Khamba ||10||

Raksha Kari Prahlad Bachayo |

Hirnakush Ko Swarg Pathayo ||11||

Lakshmi Roop Dharo Jag Mahi |

Shri Narayan Ang Samahi ||12||

Shirsindhu Mein Karat Vilaasa |

Dayasindhu Deejay Man Aasa ||13||

Hinglaaj Mein Tumhi Bhavani |

Mahima Amit Na Jaat Bakhani ||14||

Maatangi Dhumavati Mata |

Bhunvenshwari Bagla Sukh Daata ||15||

Shri Bhairav Tara Jag Taarini |

Chhin Bhaal Bhav Dukh Nivarini ||16||

Kehari Vaahan Soh Bhavani |

Laangur Beej Chalat Agvaani ||17||

Kar Mein Khappar Khadag Virajey |

Jaako Dekh Kaal Dar Bhaajey ||18||

Sohay Astra Aur Trishula |

Jaatey Uthat Shatru Hiya Shoola ||19||

Nagarkot Mein Tumhi Virajat |

Tihu Lok Mein Danka Baajat ||20||

Shumbh Nishumbh Daanav Tum Maarey

Rakt Beej Shankhan Samhaarey ||21||

Mahishasur Nrip Ati Abhimaani |

Jehi Agh Bhaar Mahi Akulani ||22||

Roop Karaal Kali Ko Dhaara |

Sen Sahit Tum Tihi Samhaara ||23||

Pari Garh Santan Par Jab Jab |

Bhayee Sahay Maatu Tum Tab Tab ||24||

Amar puri Arou sab Loka |

Tab Mahima Sab Rahe Ashoka ||25||

Jwaala Mein Hai Jyoti Tumhari |

Tumhe Sada Pujey Nar Nari ||26||

Prem Bhakti Se Jo Jas Gaavey |

Dukh Daaridra Nikat Nahi Aavey ||27||

Dhyavey Tumhe Jo Nar Man Laayee |

Janam Maran Taako Chuti Jaai ||28||

Jogi Sur Muni Kahat Pukari |

Yog Na Ho Bin Shakti Tumhari ||29||

Shankar Aacharaj Tap Kino |

Kaam Aou Krodh Jiti Sab Lino ||30||

Nishidin Dhyan dharo Shankar ko |

Kaahu Kaal Nahi Sumiro Tumko ||31||

Shakti Roop Ko Maram Na Paayo |

Shakti Gayi Tab Man Pachtaayo ||32||

Sharnagat Hui Kirti Bakhaani |

Jai Jai Jai Jagdamb Bhavani ||33||

Bhayi Prasanna Aadi Jagdamba |

Dai Shakti Nahi Kin Vilamba ||34||

Moko Maatu Kasht Ati Ghero |

Tum Bin Kaun Harey Dukh Mero ||35||

Aasha Trishna Nipat Satavey |

Moh madaadik Sab Binshavey ||36||

Shatru Naash Keejay Maharani |

Sumiro Ikchit Tumhe Bhavani ||37||

Karo Krupa Hey Maatu Dayala |

Riddhi Siddhi Dey Karahu Nihala ||38||

Jab Lagi Jiya Dayafal Paau |

Tumharo Jas May Sada Sunau ||39||

Durga Chalisa Jo Koi Gaavey |

Sab Sukh Bhog Param Padh Paavey || 40||

Devidas Sharan Nij Jaani

Karahu Kripa Jagdamb Bhavani

Sharangat Raksha Kare

Bhakt Rahe Nishank

Main Aaya Teri Sharan Mein

Maatu Lijeeye Ank.

ll Iti Sri Durga Chalisa Sampurna ll

Durga arati

Jai Ambe Gauri ,
Maiya jai Shyama Gauri
Tumko nishdin dhyavat,
Hari Brahma Shivji
Jai Ambe Gauri....

Mang sindur birajat,
tiko mrigmadko,
ujjvalse dou naina,
chandravadan niko
Jai Ambe Gauri....

Kanak saman kalevar,
raktambar raje,
Raktapushp galmala,
kanthhar saje
Jai Ambe Gauri....

Kehari vahan rajat,
khadg khappar dhari
sur nar munijan sevat,
tinke dukhahari
Jai Ambe Gauri....

Kanan kundal shobhit,
nasagre moti
Kotik chandra divakar,
samrajat jyoti
Jai Ambe Gauri....

Shumbh- nishumbh vidare,
MahishaSur ghatia
Dhumra-vilochan naina,
nishdin madmati
Jai Ambe Gauri...

Brahmani, Rudrani
tum Kamala Rani,
Agam-nigam bakhani.
turn Shiv patrani
Jai Ambe Gauri....

Chaunsath yogini gavat,
nritya karat Bhairon
Bajat tab mridanga,
aur bajat damru
Jai Ambe Gauri....

Tum ho jag ki mata,
tum hi ho bharta,
Bhaktan ki dukh harta,
sukh sampati karta
Jai Ambe Gauri....

Bhuja char ati shobhit,
var mudra dhari,
Manvanchhit phal pavat,
sevat nar nari
Jai Ambe Gauri....

Kanchan thal virajat,
agaru kapur baati shri
Maalketu men rajat,
koti ratan jyoti
Jai Ambe Gauri ,

Maiya jai Shyama Gauri
Tumko nishdin dhyavat,
Hari Brahma Shivji,
Jai Ambe Gauri....

Mantra

Om Sarvamangala Mangalye
Shive Sarvartha Sadhike
Sharanye Tryambake Gauri
Narayani Namoastute

Om Sarva Swarupe Sarveshe
Sarvashakti Samanvite
Bhayebhyastrahi No Devi
Durge Devi Namoastute

Om Jayanti Mangala Kali
Bhadrakali Kapalini.
Durga Kshama Shiva Dhatri
Swaha Swadha Namostute.

Dehi Saubhagyam Aarogyam
Dehi Me Paramam Sukham
Rupam Dehi Jayam Dehi
Yasho Dehi Dvisho Jahi

Srishti Sthiti Vinashanam
Shaktibhute Sanatani
Gunashraye Gunamaye
Narayani Namohyastu Te

Strotra

Ya Devi Sarvabhuteshu
Vishnumayeti Shabdita
Namastasyai Namastasyai
Namastasyai Namo Namah

Ya Devi Sarvabhuteshu
Chetanety Abhidhiyate
Namastasyai Namastasyai
Namastasyai Namo Namah

Ya Devi Sarvabhuteshu
Buddhirupena Samsthita
Namastasyai Namastasyai
Namastasyai Namo Namah

Ya Devi Sarvabhuteshu
Nidrarupena Samsthita
Namastasyai Namastasyai
Namastasyai Namo Namah

Ya Devi Sarvabhuteshu
Chhaya Rupena Samsthita
Namastasyai Namastasyai

Ya Devi Sarvabhuteshu
Shaktirupena Samsthita
Namastasyai Namastasyai
Namastasyai Namo Namah

Ya Devi Sarvabhuteshu
Trishnarupena Samsthita
Namastasyai Namastasyai
Namastasyai Namo Namah

Ya Devi Sarvabhuteshu
Kshantirupena Samsthita
Namastasyai Namastasyai
Namastasyai Namo Namah

Ya Devi Sarvabhuteshu
Jatirupena Samsthita
Namastasyai Namastasyai
Namastasyai Namo Namah

Ya Devi Sarvabhuteshu
Lajjarupena Samsthita
Namastasyai Namastasyai
Namastasyai Namo Namah

Ya Devi Sarvabhuteshu
Shantirupena Samsthita
Namastasyai Namastasyai
Namastasyai Namo Namah

Ya Devi Sarvabhuteshu
Shraddharupena Samsthita
Namastasyai Namastasyai
Namastasyai Namo Namah

Ya Devi Sarvabhuteshu
Kantirupena Samsthita
Namastasyai Namastasyai
Namastasyai Namo Namah

Ya Devi Sarvabhuteshu
Lakshmirupena Samsthita
Namastasyai Namastasyai
Namastasyai Namo Namah

Ya Devi Sarvabhuteshu
Vrittirupena Samsthita
Namastasyai Namastasyai
Namastasyai Namo Namah

Ya Devi Sarvabhuteshu
Smritirupena Samsthita
Namastasyai Namastasyai
Namastasyai Namo Namah

Ya Devi Sarvabhuteshu
Dayarupena Samsthita
Namastasyai Namastasyai
Namastasyai Namo Namah

Ya Devi Sarvabhuteshu
Tushtirupena Samsthita
Ya Devi Sarvabhuteshu
Matrurupena Samsthita
Namastasyai Namastasyai
Namastasyai Namo Namah

Ya Devi Sarvabhuteshu
Bhrantirupena Samsthita
Namastasyai Namastasyai
Namastasyai Namo Namah

Indriyanam Adhishtatri
Bhutanam Chakshileshu Ya
Bhuteshu Satatam Tasyai
Vyaptidevyai Namo Namah

Ya Devi Sarvabhuteshu

Smritirupena Samsthita

Namastasyai Namastasyai

Namastasyai Namo Namah

9 789334 325881

Printed at Repro India Ltd.